Bridal Shower

Guests

Name ____________________

Wishes ____________________

Advice ____________________

Name ____________________

Wishes ____________________

Advice ____________________

Guests

Name ______________________________

Wishes ______________________________

____

____

Advice ______________________________

____

____

Name ______________________________

Wishes ______________________________

____

____

Advice ______________________________

____

____

Guests

Name

Wishes

Advice

Name

Wishes

Advice

Guests

Name

Wishes

Advice

Name

Wishes

Advice

Guests

Name

Wishes

Advice

Name

Wishes

Advice

Guests

Name ______________________

Wishes ______________________

____

____

Advice ______________________

____

____

Name ______________________

Wishes ______________________

____

____

Advice ______________________

____

____

Guests
Name
Wishes
Advice
Name
Wishes
Advice

Guests

Name

Wishes

Advice

Name

Wishes

Advice

Guests

Name

Wishes

Advice

Name

Wishes

Advice

Guests

Name ______________________

Wishes ______________________

____

____

Advice ______________________

____

____

Name ______________________

Wishes ______________________

____

____

Advice ______________________

____

____

Guests

Name

Wishes

Advice

Name

Wishes

Advice

Guests

Name ______________________

Wishes ______________________

____

____

Advice ______________________

____

____

Name ______________________

Wishes ______________________

____

____

Advice ______________________

____

____

Guests

Name ______________________

Wishes ______________________

____

____

Advice ______________________

____

____

Name ______________________

Wishes ______________________

____

____

Advice ______________________

____

____

Guests

Name ______________________________

Wishes ______________________________

____

____

Advice ______________________________

____

____

Name ______________________________

Wishes ______________________________

____

____

Advice ______________________________

____

____

Guests

Name ______________________

Wishes ______________________

____

____

Advice ______________________

____

____

Name ______________________

Wishes ______________________

____

____

Advice ______________________

____

____

Guests

Name

Wishes

Advice

Name

Wishes

Advice

Guests

Name

Wishes

Advice

Name

Wishes

Advice

Guests

Name

Wishes

Advice

Name

Wishes

Advice

Guests

Name ______________________

Wishes ______________________

____

____

Advice ______________________

____

____

Name ______________________

Wishes ______________________

____

____

Advice ______________________

____

____

Guests

Name

Wishes

Advice

Name

Wishes

Advice

Guests
Name
Wishes
Advice
Name
Wishes
Advice

Guests

Name ____________________

Wishes ____________________

____

____

Advice ____________________

____

____

Name ____________________

Wishes ____________________

____

____

Advice ____________________

____

____

Guests

Name

Wishes

Advice

Name

Wishes

Advice

Guests

Name ______________________

Wishes ______________________

____

____

Advice ______________________

____

____

Name ______________________

Wishes ______________________

____

____

Advice ______________________

____

____

Guests

Name

Wishes

Advice

Name

Wishes

Advice

Guests

Name

Wishes

Advice

Name

Wishes

Advice

Guests

Name

Wishes

Advice

Name

Wishes

Advice

Guests

Name

Wishes

Advice

Name

Wishes

Advice

Guests

Name ______________________________

Wishes ______________________________

____

____

Advice ______________________________

____

____

Name ______________________________

Wishes ______________________________

____

____

Advice ______________________________

____

____

Guests

Name

Wishes

Advice

Name

Wishes

Advice

Guests

Name

Wishes

Advice

Name

Wishes

Advice

Guests

Name ______________________________

Wishes ______________________________

____

____

Advice ______________________________

____

____

Name ______________________________

Wishes ______________________________

____

____

Advice ______________________________

____

____

Guests

Name

Wishes

Advice

Name

Wishes

Advice

Guests

Name

Wishes

Advice

Name

Wishes

Advice

Guests

Name ______________________________

Wishes ______________________________

____

____

Advice ______________________________

____

____

Name ______________________________

Wishes ______________________________

____

____

Advice ______________________________

____

____

Guests

Name

Wishes

Advice

Name

Wishes

Advice

Guests

Name ____________________

Wishes ____________________

____

____

Advice ____________________

____

____

Name ____________________

Wishes ____________________

____

____

Advice ____________________

____

____

Guests

Name

Wishes

Advice

Name

Wishes

Advice

Guests
Name
Wishes
Advice
Name
Wishes
Advice

Guests

Name

Wishes

Advice

Name

Wishes

Advice

Guests

Name ______________________________

Wishes ______________________________

____

____

Advice ______________________________

____

____

Name ______________________________

Wishes ______________________________

____

____

Advice ______________________________

____

____

Guests

Name

Wishes

Advice

Name

Wishes

Advice

Guests

Name ____________________

Wishes ____________________

____

____

Advice ____________________

____

____

Name ____________________

Wishes ____________________

____

____

Advice ____________________

____

____

Guests

Name

Wishes

Advice

Name

Wishes

Advice

Guests

Name ____________________

Wishes ____________________

____

____

Advice ____________________

____

____

Name ____________________

Wishes ____________________

____

____

Advice ____________________

____

____

Guests

Name ______________________________

Wishes ______________________________

____

____

Advice ______________________________

____

____

Name ______________________________

Wishes ______________________________

____

____

Advice ______________________________

____

____

Guests

Name ___

Wishes ___

___

___

Advice ___

___

___

Name ___

Wishes ___

___

___

Advice ___

___

___

Guests

Name

Wishes

Advice

Name

Wishes

Advice

Guests

Name ______________________

Wishes ______________________

____

____

Advice ______________________

____

____

Name ______________________

Wishes ______________________

____

____

Advice ______________________

____

____

Guests

Name

Wishes

Advice

Name

Wishes

Advice

Guests
Name
Wishes
Advice
Name
Wishes
Advice

Guests

Name ______________________________

Wishes ______________________________

____

____

Advice ______________________________

____

____

Name ______________________________

Wishes ______________________________

____

____

Advice ______________________________

____

____

Guests

Name

Wishes

Advice

Name

Wishes

Advice

Guests

Name

Wishes

Advice

Name

Wishes

Advice

Guests

Name ______

Wishes ______

______

______

Advice ______

______

______

Name ______

Wishes ______

______

______

Advice ______

______

______

Guests

Name ____________________

Wishes ____________________

____

____

Advice ____________________

____

____

Name ____________________

Wishes ____________________

____

____

Advice ____________________

____

____

Guests

Name

Wishes

Advice

Name

Wishes

Advice

Guests

Name

Wishes

Advice

Name

Wishes

Advice

Guests

Name

Wishes

Advice

Name

Wishes

Advice

Guests

Name

Wishes

Advice

Name

Wishes

Advice

Guests

Name ______________________

Wishes ______________________

____

____

Advice ______________________

____

____

Name ______________________

Wishes ______________________

____

____

Advice ______________________

____

____

Guests

Name

Wishes

Advice

Name

Wishes

Advice

Guests
Name
Wishes
Advice
Name
Wishes
Advice

Guests

Name

Wishes

Advice

Name

Wishes

Advice

Guests

Name

Wishes

Advice

Name

Wishes

Advice

Guests

Name

Wishes

Advice

Name

Wishes

Advice

Guests

Name ____________________

Wishes ____________________

____

____

Advice ____________________

____

____

Name ____________________

Wishes ____________________

____

____

Advice ____________________

____

____

Guests

Name ______________________________

Wishes ______________________________

____

____

Advice ______________________________

____

____

Name ______________________________

Wishes ______________________________

____

____

Advice ______________________________

____

____

Guests

Name

Wishes

Advice

Name

Wishes

Advice

Guests

Name

Wishes

Advice

Name

Wishes

Advice

Guests

Name

Wishes

Advice

Name

Wishes

Advice

Guests

Name

Wishes

Advice

Name

Wishes

Advice

Guests

Name ________________________

Wishes ________________________

____

____

Advice ________________________

____

____

Name ________________________

Wishes ________________________

____

____

Advice ________________________

____

____

Guests

Name

Wishes

Advice

Name

Wishes

Advice

Guests
Name
Wishes
Advice
Name
Wishes
Advice

Guests

Name

Wishes

Advice

Name

Wishes

Advice

Guests

Name ______________________

Wishes ______________________

____

____

Advice ______________________

____

____

Name ______________________

Wishes ______________________

____

____

Advice ______________________

____

____

Guests

Name

Wishes

Advice

Name

Wishes

Advice

Guests

Name ______________________

Wishes ______________________

____

____

Advice ______________________

____

____

Name ______________________

Wishes ______________________

____

____

Advice ______________________

____

____

Guests

Name

Wishes

Advice

Name

Wishes

Advice

Guests

Name

Wishes

Advice

Name

Wishes

Advice

Guests

Name

Wishes

Advice

Name

Wishes

Advice

Guests

Name ________________

Wishes ________________

____

____

Advice ________________

____

____

Name ________________

Wishes ________________

____

____

Advice ________________

____

____

Guests

Name

Wishes

Advice

Name

Wishes

Advice

Guests

Name ______________________

Wishes ______________________

____

____

Advice ______________________

____

____

Name ______________________

Wishes ______________________

____

____

Advice ______________________

____

____

Guests

Name

Wishes

Advice

Name

Wishes

Advice

Guests

Name

Wishes

Advice

Name

Wishes

Advice

Guests

Name

Wishes

Advice

Name

Wishes

Advice

Guests

Name

Wishes

Advice

Name

Wishes

Advice

Guests

Name

Wishes

Advice

Name

Wishes

Advice

Guests

Name

Wishes

Advice

Name

Wishes

Advice

Guests

Name ______________________

Wishes ______________________

____

____

Advice ______________________

____

____

Name ______________________

Wishes ______________________

____

____

Advice ______________________

____

____

Guests

Name

Wishes

Advice

Name

Wishes

Advice

Guests

Name

Wishes

Advice

Name

Wishes

Advice

Guests
Name
Wishes
Advice
Name
Wishes
Advice

Guests

Name ______________________

Wishes ______________________

____

____

Advice ______________________

____

____

Name ______________________

Wishes ______________________

____

____

Advice ______________________

____

____

Guests
Name
Wishes
Advice
Name
Wishes
Advice

Guests

Name

Wishes

Advice

Name

Wishes

Advice

Guests

Name

Wishes

Advice

Name

Wishes

Advice

Guests

Name

Wishes

Advice

Name

Wishes

Advice

Gift Log

Gift Log

Gift Received	Given By	Thank You Notice Sent

Gift Log

Gift Received	Given By	Thank You Notice Sent

Gift Log

Gift Received	Given By	Thank You Notice Sent

Gift Log

Gift Received	Given By	Thank You Notice Sent

Gift Log

Gift Received	Given By	Thank You Notice Sent

Gift Log
Gift Received
Given By
Thank You Notice Sent

Gift Log
Gift Received
Given By
Thank You Notice Sent

Gift Log

Gift Received	Given By	Thank You Notice Sent

Gift Log

Gift Received	Given By	Thank You Notice Sent

Gift Log

Gift Received	Given By	Thank You Notice Sent

Gift Log

Gift Received	Given By	Thank You Notice Sent

Gift Log

Gift Received	Given By	Thank You Notice Sent

Gift Log
Gift Received
Given By
Thank You Notice Sent

Gift Log

Gift Received	Given By	Thank You Notice Sent

Gift Log
Gift Received
Given By
Thank You Notice Sent

Gift Log

Gift Received	Given By	Thank You Notice Sent

Made in United States
Orlando, FL
23 March 2022

16042844R00067